Contents

Introduction

The purpose of this material is to provide opportunities to check students' understanding of the *Starstruck* reading books and to provide structures to encourage writing.

Students working at the reading level assumed by this book frequently have a considerable mis-match between their experiential and oral skills and their skills of reading and writing. The *Starstruck* reading books and the support material provide materials which are:

✔ interesting,

✔ age appropriate,

✔ achievable, and

✔ appropriately challenging.

This workbook covers three *Starstruck* reading books: *Musical Theatre*, *Street Dance* and *Stage Makeup*. Each reading book in the series is supported by a selection of eight worksheets. Four worksheets support the non-fiction section and four support the fiction section. The first two worksheets for both the fiction and non-fiction material are designed for students experiencing the greatest difficulties. The second two worksheets (for both non-fiction and fiction) are more challenging in both vocabulary and content:

- Worksheet 1 – *non-fiction, lower level*
- Worksheet 2 – *non-fiction, lower level*
- Worksheet 3 – *non-fiction, higher level*
- Worksheet 4 – *non-fiction, higher level*

- Worksheet 5 – *fiction, lower level*
- Worksheet 6 – *fiction, lower level*
- Worksheet 7 – *fiction, higher level*
- Worksheet 8 – *fiction, higher level*

However, there is no repetition within the set of tasks for any individual book, which enables the teacher to use the full set to provide a degree of progression if appropriate.

Much of the vocabulary used on the worksheets is that used in the reading texts. Rubric has been kept to a minimum. Each sheet has its own section in the teacher's notes in this workbook, where the tasks are fully explained.

In a few tasks further research is suggested. Detailed suggestions have not been given, as this is predominantly dependent on the skill levels of the students. This would, obviously, be an appropriate place to use ICT.

Many of the tasks also include opportunities for oral work. Many of the open tasks also provide opportunities for display work, particularly where students are encouraged to make their own decisions about the specific content.

Musical Theatre Teacher's Notes

Worksheet 1 – True or false?

Activity: Non-fiction   **Level:**   Lower

Task: True or false – comprehension.

The worksheet invites students to consider statements, to decide whether the statements are true or false, and to explain their reasons. Students will therefore need to find evidence (from the reading book text) to support their decisions. Their explanations could be written in note form on the worksheet.

If necessary, identify the relevant reading book sections and their page numbers before students attempt the task.

In most cases the true or false decision is straightforward. Note that the final statement is false: the two gangs in the story are the Jets and the *Sharks*.

Worksheet 2 – Jobs in musical theatre

Activity: Non-fiction   **Level:**   Lower

Task: Jobs in musical theatre. Making notes.

Re-read pages 14 – 15 of the reading book ('*Jobs in musical theatre*'). Make a list of the jobs discussed in this section. Some jobs are listed in the word box on the worksheet: these can serve as a starter.

Discuss with the students whether these jobs take place onstage during the show, or are offstage (so that the individuals are not seen by the audience).

Students should then select up to six of these jobs. They should write the name of the job in the first column on the worksheet. They should then decide whether the job involves being onstage or offstage during the show and write this in the second column. The final column is to allow the students to write in some notes about what the job involves.

Explain to the students that the information is to be recorded in note form.

5

Worksheet 3 – Glossary

Activity: Non-fiction   **Level:** Higher

Task: Glossary work: to complete a glossary.

Discuss with the students what a glossary is and why glossaries are often found in non-fiction books.

Look at the words in the box at the top of the worksheet and locate them in the text of the reading book. Discuss the meaning of each of the words.

Note that in a glossary the words are given in alphabetical order.

Ask the students to choose six of the words from the box and write a glossary entry for each on the worksheet.

Worksheet 4 – Famous shows

Activity: Non-fiction   **Level:** Higher

Task: Note-making.

The worksheet requires students to complete a table about four musical theatre shows. Information about these shows can be found on pages 8 – 11 of the reading book.

The students should complete the table in note form. In the second column they should list key dates and other information relating to that show – for example, when it was first performed, performances in other countries, the number of performances, etc. This is a good opportunity for further research, for example using the Internet, where extensive information can be found.

Students may use the final column to note why the show is famous. Discuss with the students how a show can become famous. It could be because of a famous 'first' – such as the first show to land a real helicopter on stage during the performance, or the first real musical theatre show. Or it could become famous because it receives a lot of good (or bad) publicity.

The students can then fill in the table.

As an extension activity, use the students' notes in the completed table to write a short passage about one or more of the shows listed.

Worksheet 5 – Retelling the story

Activity: Fiction   **Level:** Lower

Task: To complete the synopsis of the story.

The worksheet consists of a partially completed synopsis of the story 'Dilemma'. The students are required to fill in the gaps.

There is a help box of useful words at the bottom of the worksheet. Read these words with the students. Note that not all of the words needed to complete the activity are given in the box.

Read through the synopsis with the students and ask them to suggest words or phrases to put in the gaps. If appropriate, add any words they suggest to the help box.

The students should then complete the synopsis.

Worksheet 6 – How much can you remember?

Activity: Fiction   **Level:** Lower

Task: Reading for understanding. Comprehension.

The students should write their answers to the questions on the worksheet in full sentences. However, the worksheet questions could also be used as an oral quiz.

As an extension activity, ask the students to devise more questions that could be used in a quiz.

Worksheet 7 – TV interview – Idea for the story

Activity: Fiction   **Level:** Higher

Task: To script a TV interview with Alice.

Explain to the students that, for the purposes of this worksheet, Alice's book has now been published. To promote the book, Alice is being interviewed on television.

The worksheet provides a partially completed script for this interview, which the students are required to complete.

At the end of the interview, the students are asked to come up with two final questions of their own. This is a challenging task. Note that the students will need to explain that the story is in fact the story of Alice's discussions with Kim in trying to think of a story!

Worksheet 8 – Planning a story

Activity: Fiction   **Level:** Higher

Task: To plan a story using the given template.

The template on the worksheet provides an outline for a story titled *Dance Fever*. The students are required to fill in the details of the story plan.

Talk through the main points of the story that are presented on the worksheet, i.e. the main character is a dance queen. She enters a dance competition, but needs to find a partner. She does this (*how?*) and they practise for the competition. Everything is going fine, but then something happens the day before the competition. (Perhaps one of the dancers is injured, or a costume is damaged.) The situation is resolved, and the dancers get to the competition just in time.

The students are also required to describe how the dancers fare in the competition.

This activity would be appropriate for planning in small groups, or as a class. If necessary, provide vocabulary to support the students' ideas.

The activity could be extended by asking the students to write the story.

True or false?

Some of these sentences are true, and some are not!
What do you think?

Statement	T/F	Reason
Show Boat was written by Andrew Lloyd Webber.	F	I think this because ....
The Prince of Tennis Musical is a Bollywood movie.		I think this because ....
You can go to college to study musical theatre.		I think this because ....
In **Japanese Noh theatre** the actors wear masks.		I think this because ....
The first musical theatre – **The Black Crook** – ran for five and a half hours.		I think this because ....
Broadway is in the West End of London.		I think this because ....
West Side Story is about two gangs: the Jets and the Aces.		I think this because ....

Jobs in musical theatre

Job	Onstage or offstage?	What they do

Word box

performer	musician	singer
producer	orchestra	dancer
composer	costume	money
costume designer	light	music
lighting designer	actor	

Glossary

Here are some hard words from the book. What do they mean?

stage manager	career
producer	Sanskrit drama
lyricist	the book
sabilla	choreographer
Noh theatre	director

Word	Page number	Meaning

Famous shows

Here are some famous musical theatre shows.

Fill in the table.

Show	Dates and other information	Why it is famous
Show Boat		
Oklahoma!		
West Side Story		
The Phantom of the Opera		

Retelling the story

Alice is a .... She writes .... One day a

.... asks her to ....

.... Now she has to ....

.... She asks her daughter, ..., to help.

Kim has an idea for the story. In her idea, a girl is ....

.... The girl wants

to be on .... But the girl's mum says she is too ....

Alice says this is the story for .... So she can't use it.

Kim has another idea ....

But this idea is the plot for ....

There is even a song called ....

Kim has two more ideas. One idea is the story of ....

The other idea is ....

.... Then Alice has an idea for a story.

In her idea ....

.... That's the story!

Help box

Grease Lightning	Billy Elliot	books	....
Cheeky Charlie	publisher	plump	....
writer	Grease	....	....

How much can you remember?

Who asked Alice to write a story about musical theatre?

What was Kim learning about at school?

Why did the girl want to go on the Cheeky Charlie show?

Why couldn't Alice use Kim's first idea?

In Kim's second idea, who met on holiday?

In Kim's second idea, who built a car?

Did Kim have any ideas of her own?

In the end, who had the idea for the story?

TV Interview – Idea for the story

| INTERVIEWER | : | Did anybody help you with ideas for the story? |

| ALICE | : | Well, at first I couldn't think of .... |

So I asked ....

| INTERVIEWER | : | Did she have lots of ideas? |

| ALICE | : | Yes. But the trouble was .... |

....

| INTERVIEWER | : | So what did you say to her? |

| ALICE | : | .... |

....

| INTERVIEWER | : | .... |

....

| ALICE | : | .... |

....

| INTERVIEWER | : | .... |

....

| ALICE | : | .... |

....

15

Planning a story

Fill in the information in this story plan. The title of the story is **Dance Fever**.

Chapter 1

.... is a dance queen. Every Saturday night she

.... One night she sees

a poster for a dance competition. She ....

....

Chapter 2

.... needs to find a partner. She ....

....

.... They practise hard for the competition. Everything is going

....

Chapter 3

The day before the competition, there is a disaster! ....

....

....

....

Chapter 4

.... and .... get to the competition just

in time. They ....

....

....

....

Street Dance Teacher's Notes

Worksheet 1 – Fill in the gaps

Activity: Non-fiction   **Level:** Lower

Task: A cloze activity on street dance.

The worksheet presents six incomplete sentences, based on the non-fiction section of the reading book. The students are required to complete the sentences using the appropriate words provided in the box on the worksheet.

This is a straightforward activity, though a preliminary class discussion on the various kinds of street dance and the various dance moves would probably be helpful.

Worksheet 2 – What am I doing?

Activity: Non-fiction   **Level:** Lower

Task: To match sentence starts and ends to create a report.

The worksheet consists of jumbled-up sentence starts (in column one) and sentence endings (in column two). Read through each sentence start and ask the students to identify which ending is most appropriate. To make the task more challenging, you could cover the sentence endings and ask the students to suggest appropriate endings instead.

The complete sentences are:

> When a dancer pops, they jerk their body quickly.
> Breakdancing is one kind of street dance.
> Street dance has no rules: you can dance any way you want to.
> When a dancer freezes in one position, it's called a lock.
> When a dancer makes energetic movements, it's called krumping.
> You won't see street dance in concert halls or theatres.
> Roboting is dancing like a robot.
> In Japan you can see street dance every Sunday in Yoyogi Park in Tokyo.
> Dance battles are an important part of street dance.
> B-boying started in New York City, in the USA, in the 1970s.

Worksheet 3 – Street Dance web site

Activity: Non-fiction   **Level:** Higher

Task: To complete a home page for a web site on street dance.

The worksheet is a skeleton for a web site home page on street dance. Discuss the idea of a web site on street dance with the students. What would somebody visiting such a web site want to know or do? Make a list of the kinds of things that the web site might cover. This might include:

- information about kinds of street dance and dance moves;

- listings of dance battles that are happening soon;

- video clips and photographs of street dance – possibly submitted by visitors to the site;

- information on how to get started as a street dancer.

Talk through the sections on the worksheet with the students, before they begin their own writing in the spaces provided.

Worksheet 4 – Magazine article

Activity: Non-fiction   **Level:** Higher

Task: To write an article on dance battles.

Explain that the task is to produce an article about dance battles for a monthly magazine, using the question and answer framework provided on the worksheet.

Explain that the answers should be presented using full sentences. Encourage the students to add any additional ideas of their own. If necessary, model an appropriate example answer for the first question.

The final question in the worksheet article is more open-ended and is not covered in the reading book. This is an opportunity for creative writing.

As an alternative, ask the students to produce this information as a web page on dance battle tips.

Worksheet 5 – Kelly's text messages

Activity: Fiction **Level:** Lower

Task: To devise text messages as a means of telling the story.

The worksheet asks the students to reduce certain events of the story to short text messages, of no more than 100 characters each, sent by Kelly to her friends. There is one example answer, to assist the students in understanding the task.

Ensure that the students understand that text message 'characters' include individual letters, spaces and punctuation marks. If the students are adept at texting they may be able to abbreviate their words, thus using fewer characters.

Explain that GR8!, in the example text message, stands for 'Great!'.

Worksheet 6 – Picture briefs

Activity: Fiction **Level:** Lower

Task: To write picture briefs.

The worksheet explains about picture briefs and asks the students to write two briefs. Ensure that the students have grasped the idea of the picture brief. An example is given on the worksheet.

The two pictures on the worksheet are taken from the story in the reading book. Explain that only an outline description is required for each – a couple of sentences will suffice, as artists are expected to use their imagination to fill in the details.

Worksheet 7 – Kelly's mum's diary

Activity: Fiction   **Level:** Higher

Task: Writing in the first person – creative writing.

The worksheet comprises two extracts from Kelly's mum's diary, for students to complete. For both diary entries, the students are required to record the events of the day, together with a summary of how Kelly's mum would feel in each case.

Discuss what happened, using the prompts on the worksheet. Discuss how Kelly's mum would feel and react. Encourage the students to put the information in their own words, rather than just copying chunks from the text.

Note that for the first diary entry, we know from the story that Kelly's mum went to the school to wait for Kelly, and we know that Kelly was not there. But the students will have to infer what Kelly's mum's reaction was in this situation.

The final section of the worksheet (at the park) allows scope for creative writing – taking the story on to a new stage. Bob tells Kelly's mum that she is a good dancer. Discuss what Kelly's mum is likely to do in this situation. Extend the writing on to another sheet if required.

As an extension activity, students could be asked to continue the story along these lines.

Worksheet 8 – An extra chapter

Activity: Fiction   **Level:** Higher

Task: To plan an extra chapter for the story.

Students are asked to imagine that Kelly's mum decides to enter more dance battles, after her dance at the park. The students are required to write a plan for this extra chapter, on the worksheet. The key issues in writing this are:

- Kelly's mum finds that she is good at street dance. How can she enter more dance battles? Students will need to think about how the story develops.

- What does Kelly think about her mum's activities? At the end of the story we get the feeling that Kelly is embarrassed by her mum.

As an extension, ask the students to write out in full one section of the planned chapter. Alternatively the students could write the whole chapter, if appropriate.

Fill in the gaps

Find the right word from the box to fill in the gaps below

judges	YouTube	exercise
b-girls	battle	freezes
nightclubs	raves	b-boys
Jumpstyle	movies	
lock	breakers	

1. .... started at raves and dance clubs in Belgium.

2. Hip-hop dancers are called ....,

   .... or ....

3. When a dancer .... in one position, it's called a

   ....

4. In a dance ...., ...

   .... decide who is the winner.

5. You can see street dance on ...., in the

   ...., in ....

   and at ....

6. Street dance is good ....

What am I doing?

When a dancer pops …	… you can dance any way you want to.
Breakdancing is …	… it's called a lock.
Street dance has no rules: …	… dancing like a robot.
When a dancer freezes in one position …	… one kind of street dance.
When a dancer makes energetic movements …	… started in New York City, in the USA, in the 1970s.
You won't see street dance …	… they jerk their body quickly.
Roboting is …	… it's called krumping.
In Japan you can see street dance …	… are an important part of street dance.
Dance battles …	… in concert halls or theatres.
B-boying …	… every Sunday in Yoyogi Park in Tokyo.

Street Dance

http://www.streetdance.com

iGoogle

Google

Welcome to a web site about street dance.

What is street dance?

- ....
- ....
- ....

Dance moves:

- ....
- ....
- ....

- ....
- ....
- ....
- ....
- ....

Magazine article

Street magazine

Our street fashion editor, Grace Young, answers questions about **street dance battles**.

Q What are dance battles?

A
....
....
....

Q Who takes part in the battles?

A
....
....
....

Q Who decides the winner?

A
....
....
....

Q How do I organise a dance battle?

A
....
....
....

24

Kelly's text messages

Kelly likes to send text messages to her friends to let them know what she is up to. The messages are always short – no more than 100 characters each!

Can you write Kelly's texts at these points in the story?

The first one is done for you.

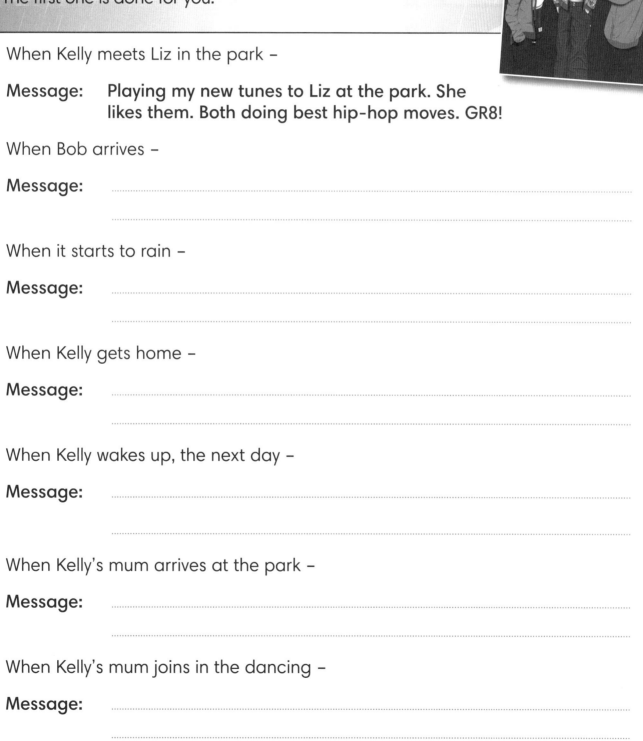

When Kelly meets Liz in the park –

Message: Playing my new tunes to Liz at the park. She likes them. Both doing best hip-hop moves. GR8!

When Bob arrives –

Message: ....

....

When it starts to rain –

Message: ....

....

When Kelly gets home –

Message: ....

....

When Kelly wakes up, the next day –

Message: ....

....

When Kelly's mum arrives at the park –

Message: ....

....

When Kelly's mum joins in the dancing –

Message: ....

....

Picture briefs

The author of a story has to tell the artist what should go in the pictures. This is called a picture brief.

Here is a picture brief for the picture on page 29:

Kelly is walking upstairs. Her mum is standing at the bottom of the stairs. Her mum wants to know where Kelly has been.

Now write the picture briefs for these two pictures.

Kelly's mum's diary

DIARY FRIDAY

Today I went to Kelly's school to wait for her. But ....

....

....

Later, Kelly came home. I asked her where she had been. ....

....

....

....

....

DIARY SATURDAY

Early this morning I went to Kelly's room. She ....

....

....

So I drove to the park. When I got there ....

....

....

....

An extra chapter

'Hey you're good!' Bob said to Kelly's mum.
'I think you should win the battle,' he said.

At the end of the story Kelly's mum is in a dance battle with Bob. He tells her she should win the battle.

Use this sheet to plan an extra chapter for the story. In this chapter Kelly's mum decides to enter more dance battles. She practises hard. Kelly helps her.

Think of a good ending for the chapter. Kelly's mum could win the battles. Or maybe she meets Bob's mother or father in the final battle (maybe they are dancers too).

Chapter Five

....

....

....

....

....

....

....

....

....

....

....

....

....

Stage Makeup Teacher's Notes

Worksheet 1 – Special effects makeup

Activity: Non-fiction   **Level:** Lower

Task: To produce a design for special effects makeup on a face.

Explain that the task is to produce a design for special effects makeup for a film or a play. The students can decide what kind of character they are preparing the design for (e.g. it could be a fantasy or horror creature, or somebody who is much older than the actor). Discuss the various ways in which faces can be made up using special effects.

Ask the students to consider their design and then to draw it on the blank face on the worksheet. They may like to add an appropriate hairstyle. The students should then complete a design brief. This should begin with a written description of their design, including details such as the materials needed to produce it.

Finally, ask the students to assess the effectiveness of their design, in the space provided on the worksheet. Alternatively, they could comment on another student's design and brief.

Worksheet 2 – Film and TV makeup

Activity: Non-fiction   **Level:** Lower

Task: A cloze exercise, followed by a sentence completion activity.

The worksheet presents a partially completed report about film and TV makeup, and requires the students to fill in the gaps, using the words provided in the help box. There is then a sentence to complete.

Re-read the non-fiction section of the reading book. Discuss with the students how makeup for film and TV is different from makeup for the theatre, for example, based on the students' readings of the text. Review the worksheet and ensure that the students understand the meanings of the words in the help box. Note that there is one answer provided for each blank on the sheet.

The completed text is:

> Makeup for film and TV is not like makeup for the theatre. In the theatre the actor is quite far away.

29

In a film the actor may be both indoors and outdoors.
The film will have all kinds of shots.
The makeup must look natural. It must also be perfect.
Bad makeup will show up easily!

Point out that the final sentence activity on the worksheet is to be completed in the students' own words. The students are required to identify one other way in which film and TV makeup differs from makeup for the theatre. This task could initially be undertaken as an oral group activity. The task could be extended by writing a more substantial piece of explanatory text.

Worksheet 3 – Makeup tips and tricks

Activity: Non-fiction   **Level:**   Higher

Task: Instructional writing.

The students are asked to imagine that they are an expert on stage makeup. Here they are giving instruction to a new assistant, using information from the reading book. Ensure that the students are familiar with the format of instructional writing and the use of the imperative.

The most straightforward task would be to instruct the assistant in understanding the differences between makeup for the stage and makeup for film and television. Alternatively, they might prefer to focus on specific stage makeup tips and tricks that are outlined in the book (pages 12 – 13).

It may be helpful to ask the students to prepare for the writing by listing the points they wish to make, in note form, before they begin.

Worksheet 4 – The best stage makeup you can buy

Activity: Non-fiction   **Level:**   Higher

Task: To design a poster advertising a stage makeup product.

The worksheet asks students to complete the design of a poster for a new product used for stage makeup.

Work with the class to generate ideas for the kinds of product it could be. Obviously it could be a type of makeup, but it could be a makeup remover, or something used in special effects makeup. Encourage the students to be inventive in their ideas: it could, for example, be a mysterious new product to make all makeup look better under stage lights, or last longer.

Once the students have decided on the product, they will need to think about how best to advertise it on the poster. What features would make stage makeup artists most want to buy it? If appropriate, make a list on the board.

Students should then complete their posters. This could be done on the worksheet, or as an ICT activity.

Worksheet 5 – Design a poster

Activity: Fiction   **Level:** Lower

Task: To design a poster to let everyone know about the fancy dress competition.

The worksheet shows a blank poster for the fancy dress competition featured in the story. Students are required to design and complete the poster.

First, discuss with the class the information that would need to go on the poster. On the board, list useful words to help the students design the poster. Discuss whether other information needs to be included on the poster – e.g. suggestions for characters etc. to dress up as.

The students can then design their posters. The posters could also be produced as an ICT activity.

Worksheet 6 – Understanding the story

Activity: Fiction   **Level:** Lower

Task: To demonstrate understanding of the story.

Most of the questions on the worksheet are straightforward. However, the last question (why the alien thought they gave prizes for strange things) may require class discussion. Did the alien know that it was a fancy dress competition? Or did she think the prize was for being the best alien? The answer is not necessarily clear from the story.

Ask the students to write down their answers in complete sentences.

Worksheet 7 – Play script

Activity: Fiction   **Level:** Higher

Task: To write a play script.

The worksheet asks the students to imagine the scene after the fancy dress party and after the alien has (unknown to Rose and Jordan) returned to her home planet. Rose and Jordan still need to decide which of them is the better makeup artist.

The students should write an appropriate play script.

Pose the questions below to the group. Note their answers and suggestions on the board.

- Why did the fancy dress competition fail to find the best makeup artist?

- What kind of thing could Jordan and Rose do next? They could, for example, ask Milly or some of the actors to decide on the best makeup artist.

- If there is a 'winner', is the other person likely to accept the decision?

- What might happen next?

Worksheet 8 – Two blogs

Activity: Fiction   **Level:** Higher

Task: Personal writing.

There are two blogs to be completed on the worksheet. The first is by Rose, describing what happened at the fancy dress competition. This blog should be written as if she is writing it on the morning after the competition.

Discuss what Rose would want to tell her friends on her blog. She would no doubt recount the events of the evening, but she would also probably describe her feelings. How would she be feeling? List ideas on the board, before the students complete the blog.

The second blog to be completed is by the alien, written after she returns to her home planet. Discuss how the alien would be feeling, having won the prize.

The students should then briefly describe the events from the alien's point of view, in the blog.

Special effects makeup

Design Brief

The character:

....

....

....

....

....

....

Description of finished design:

....

....

....

....

....

....

Materials needed:

....

....

....

....

....

Other information:

....

....

....

....

....

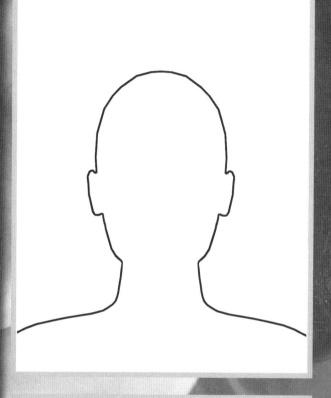

Comment

I think my design is good

because ....

....

....

....

....

....

....

....

....

Film and TV makeup

Fill in the gaps in this report:

Makeup for film and TV is not like makeup for the ....

In the theatre the .... is ....

In a film the actor may be both .... and ....

....

The film will have all kinds of ....

The makeup must look ....

It must also be ....

.... will show up easily!

Finish this sentence in your own words:

Makeup for film and TV is also different because ....

....

....

....

....

Help Box

theatre	shots	quite far away
perfect	natural	bad makeup
indoors	actor	outdoors

Makeup tips and tricks

I am going to tell you some stage makeup tips and tricks. These are used by the experts!

First

The best stage makeup you can buy

There is some great new stage makeup that you can buy.

Finish off this poster advert for the makeup.

The best stage makeup you can buy

Looks great!

- ....
  ....

- ....
  ....

- ....
  ....

- ....
  ....

- ....
  ....

Special offer!

- ....
  ....
  ....

Design a poster

Design a poster to let everyone know about the fancy dress competition.
Make sure it tells people everything they need to know.

Fancy Dress Competition

....

....

....

....

Where: ....

When: ....

- ....
- ....
- ....
- ....

....

....

....

....

Understanding the story

Chapter One

Who was fed up with the arguing?

_____

Who decided to have a competition?

_____

Chapter Two

Who decided what kind of competition it should be?

_____

Why did everybody love their makeup?

_____

_____

Chapter Three

Who won the fancy dress competition?

_____

Why were Rose and Jordan worried?

_____

Chapter Four

Did they find out who was the best makeup artist?

_____

Why did the alien think they gave prizes for strange things?

_____

_____

38

Play script

The best makeup artist

Jordan and Rose need to decide which of them is the better makeup artist. The fancy dress competition did not do this.

What will they do next?

JORDAN: We still need to find out who is the best makeup artist. How do we do this?

ROSE: I have a good idea! We could ....

....

....

JORDAN: ....

....

....

..............: ....

....

..............: ....

....

..............: ....

....

Two blogs

ROSE'S BLOG   SUNDAY March 6th

Last night I went to a fancy dress party. There was a competition and a prize for the winner. Jordan and I did the makeup for the fancy dress. But then a strange thing happened. ....

....

....

....

....

....

0 COMMENTS
LABELS: PARTY, COMPETITION, PUZZLE

THE ALIEN'S BLOG   MOONDAY plus 4

Last night I went to a fancy dress party. There was a competition and a prize for the winner. Guess what? I won!

But the thing is, I don't know ....

....

....

....

....

0 COMMENTS
LABELS: PARTY, WINNER, PLANET EARTH